4/2013
ACPL Laramie, WY
39092083442352
Malam, John,
Journey of a book /

WITHDRAWN

W9-CUC-054

Albany County Public
Library
Sources of Materials
FY12

■ County Sales Tax
■ City Sales Tax
■ Foundation
■ Friends
■ Cash Gifts from Public
■ Replacement Fees
■ Donated Items

Journey of a Book

John Malam

Heinemann
LIBRARY

Chicago, Illinois

Albany County
Public Library
Laramie, Wyoming

www.capstonepub.com
Visit our website to find out more information about Heinemann-Raintree books.

To order:
☎ Phone 800-747-4992
▭ Visit www.capstonepub.com to browse our catalog and order online.

© 2013 Heinemann Library
an imprint of Capstone Global Library, LLC
Chicago, Illinois

All rights reserved. No part of this publication may be reproduced or transmitted in any form or by any means, electronic or mechanical, including photocopying, recording, taping, or any information storage and retrieval system, without permission in writing from the publisher.

Edited by Dan Nunn and Diyan Leake
Designed by Cynthia Della-Rovere
Original illustrations © Capstone Global Library Ltd 2013
Illustrated by Capstone Global Library Ltd
Picture research by Mica Brancic
Production by Alison Parsons

Originated by Capstone Global Library Ltd
Printed and bound in China by Leo Paper Products Ltd

16 15 14 13 12
10 9 8 7 6 5 4 3 2 1

Cataloging-in-Publication Data is available at the Library of Congress website.
ISBN: 978-1-4329-6600-3 (HB)
ISBN: 978-1-4329-6607-2 (PB)

Acknowledgments

The author and publishers are grateful to the following for permission to reproduce copyright material: © Capstone Global Library Ltd (Lord and Leverett) pp. 1, 3, 4, 9, 10, 11, 12, 14, 15, 17, 18, 19, 29 top, 31; © Capstone Publishers (Karon Dubke) p. 16; Corbis pp. 5 (Blend Images/© Shannon Fagan), 28 (Zefa/© Matthias Tunger), 29 bottom (Blend Images/© Shannon Fagan); Doug Parsons p. 27; Getty Images (Radius Images) p. 6; © Leo Paper Products pp. 21, 22, 23, 24, 25; Shutterstock pp. 7 (© Goodluz), 26 (© J. van der Wolf).

Cover photograph of a pile of books and photograph of a library of books reproduced with permission of © Capstone Global Library Ltd (Lord & Leverett); photograph of a notebook for notes with horizontal stripes reproduced with permission of Shutterstock (© Matti).

Every effort has been made to contact copyright holders of material reproduced in this book. Any omissions will be rectified in subsequent printings if notice is given to the publisher.

Disclaimer

All the Internet addresses (URLs) given in this book were valid at the time of going to press. However, due to the dynamic nature of the Internet, some addresses may have changed, or sites may have changed or ceased to exist since publication. While the author and publisher regret any inconvenience this may cause readers, no responsibility for any such changes can be accepted by either the author or the publisher.

Contents

Some words are shown in bold, **like this**. You can find out what they mean by looking in the Glossary.

What Will You Read?

It's good to read a book! It could be a comic book, a poetry book, a joke book, a pop-up book, or a **fiction** book. The book in your hands right now is a **nonfiction** book.

There are so many books to choose from!

I wonder how my book was made.

Have you ever wondered how a book is made? Where do the ideas come from? How do the pictures get onto the pages? A book has an interesting journey on its way to your bookshelves, as you are about to find out.

It's All About Teamwork

It takes a lot of people to make a book. They work together as a team. Each person on the team does a different job. Little by little, the book comes together.

Everyone on the team does a different job.

These are some of the people on the team that makes a book: **author**, **editor**, **illustrator**, **picture researcher**, **photographer**, and **designer**. You will find out about them in this book.

Good Ideas

A book starts with someone having a good idea. If it is a **fiction** book, the idea usually comes from an **author**. The author sends the idea to a **publishing company**. If the company likes the author's idea, it might turn it into a book.

This author is going to mail in her fiction book idea.

The editor describes a nonfiction book idea.

If it is a **nonfiction** book, it is usually an **editor** who has the idea for it. The editor works for the publishing company. He or she asks an author to write the book.

Author and Editor

The editor talks to the author about the book.

Authors work with **editors**. For a **fiction** book, the author and editor will talk about the story. The editor might make suggestions. This could be very helpful for the author. For a **nonfiction** book, the editor tells the author what the book should be like.

The editor of this book told the author that the book should have 32 pages. He said there should be two to four sentences on each page. He also said what age the book should be for (your age), and whether it should have photographs or **illustrations**.

This author is talking to her editor about her book.

Writing an Outline

The **author** writes an outline, or plan, for the book. This sets out what will be in the book, from beginning to end. It helps the author to write the book. It also tells the **editor** what the author is going to write about.

An outline is a list of ideas.

FEARSOME FORCES OF NATURE - Bookplan

Pages 4-5
What are forces of nature?
Introduction to forces of nature. Explain what they are.

Pages 6-7 and 8-9
Violent volcanoes
Talk about what volcanoes are and how they erupt. Mention famous volcanoes.

Pages 10-11 and 12-13
Terrible earthquakes
Explain about earthquakes and how/where they happen. Mention 2011 Japan earthquake.

Pages 14-15
Walls of water
What are tsunamis and how/where do they occur? Famous tsunamis.

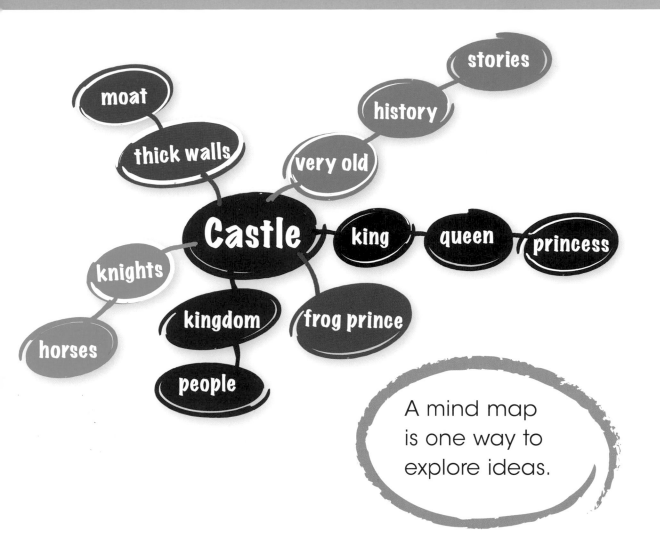

moat

thick walls

very old

history

stories

Castle

king

queen

princess

knights

kingdom

frog prince

horses

people

A mind map is one way to explore ideas.

Fiction authors have a good **imagination**. Their outline shows the ideas they have for their story. **Nonfiction** authors are good at finding information. Their outline shows the facts they will write about.

Writing the Book

The **author** writes the book, following the outline or plan as closely as possible. Most authors type their books onto a computer. Some authors write their books on paper, then type them up.

This author is writing her book.

The editor is the first person to read the book.

When the author finishes writing the book, he or she sends it to another **editor**. The editor reads it very carefully. Sometimes the editor asks the author to make changes or to double-check facts.

Photographs and Illustrations

A **nonfiction** book usually has photographs in it. A person called a **picture researcher** finds the photographs. The picture researcher might borrow the photographs from a picture library. A **photographer** might take some photographs for the book.

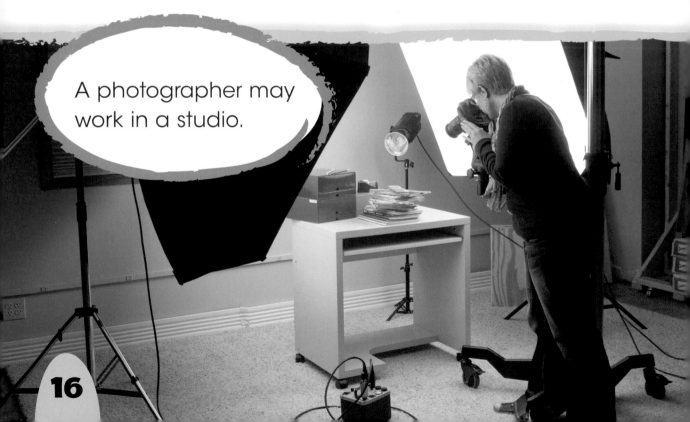

A photographer may work in a studio.

This illustrator is adding color to an illustration.

Fiction books often have **illustrations**. Some nonfiction books do, too. **Illustrators** first do their drawings in pencil. Then, they color them in with felt-tip pens, pencil crayons, or paints. Some illustrators use computers to make their pictures.

Laying Out the Pages

Every book needs a **designer**. Designers decide where to place the words, photographs, and **illustrations** of a book. They also choose which **font** to use for the letters and what colors to use for backgrounds.

This designer is using a scanner to get an illustration onto a computer.

computer

scanner

The designer is figuring out where to put the words and pictures on a page.

Designers lay out books on a computer, page by page. They move the words and pictures around on the computer screen until they are in the best place. They make sure everything looks good.

To the Printer

After the **designer** has finished laying out the book, it is ready for printing. Books are printed in **factories** all over the world. This book was printed in China. You can see the name of the **printing company** on the second page of this book.

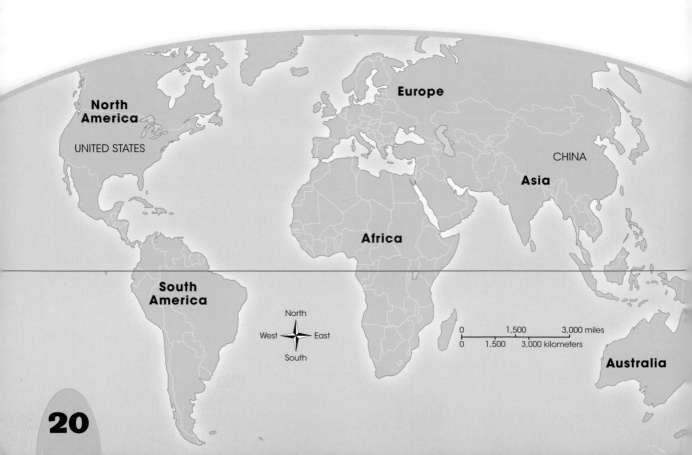

North America
UNITED STATES
Europe
CHINA
Asia
Africa
South America
North
West — East
South
0   1,500   3,000 miles
0   1,500   3,000 kilometers
Australia

The printing company is in a big building.

The **publishing company** sends the book to the printing company over the Internet. The printer gets the cover and pages with all the words and pictures in place. They are exactly the way the designer created them.

Ink on Paper

There are lots of machines doing different jobs inside the printing **factory**. Printing machines use several colors of ink to print the words and pictures of the book.

It is noisy and hot inside a printing factory. There is a strong smell of printing ink.

Printing machines are very big.

Sometimes paper for printing books comes in big, flat sheets. Sometimes it comes off a huge roll in one long strip. The paper has lots of pages from the book printed on it.

Folding, Cutting, and Binding

When the ink is dry, machines fold the paper. They fold until the paper is the size of the book pages. Then, machines cut the paper to make the page edges neat.

Look how much paper this machine cuts through at a time!

This machine makes book covers out of thick cardboard.

The pages are sent to the bindery. This is where the book cover is bound, or joined, to the inside pages. The book is then finished. The printing **factory** makes thousands of copies of the book.

Transporting the Books

The finished books are packed into large cardboard boxes. The boxes are sent to the **publishing company**. They travel by ship and truck.

Big ships carry metal containers filled with books.

The publishing company stores the books in its **warehouse**. The books go from the warehouse to libraries, schools, bookstores, and other kinds of stores.

Ready to Read!

Customers pay the stores for the books. The stores buy the books from the **publishing company**. The publishing company uses the money to pay the printer and the team of people who made the book.

It is fun to choose a new book to read.

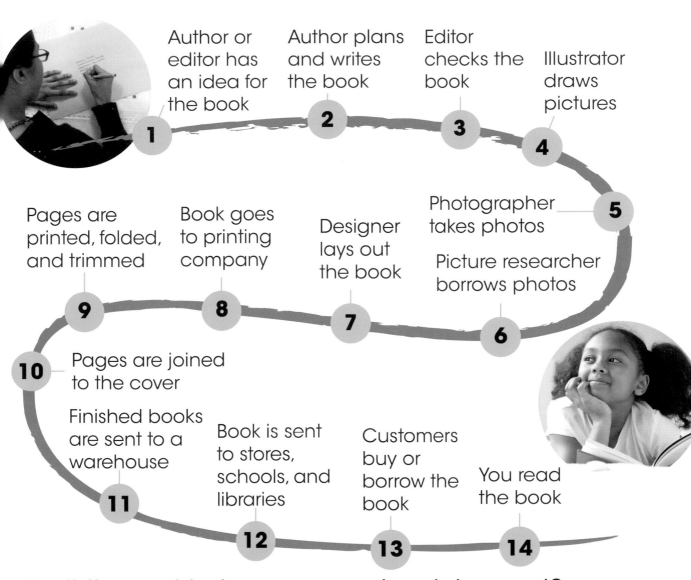

1. Author or editor has an idea for the book

2. Author plans and writes the book

3. Editor checks the book

4. Illustrator draws pictures

5. Photographer takes photos

6. Picture researcher borrows photos

7. Designer lays out the book

8. Book goes to printing company

9. Pages are printed, folded, and trimmed

10. Pages are joined to the cover

11. Finished books are sent to a warehouse

12. Book is sent to stores, schools, and libraries

13. Customers buy or borrow the book

14. You read the book

Isn't it good to have a new book to read? Just think, your favorite **author** is probably writing a new book right now—but you will have to wait to read it!

Glossary

author person who writes the words for a book

designer person who lays out the words and pictures for the pages of a book

editor person who works with an author, checking what he or she has written

factory building where things are made

fiction type of writing that describes imaginary people and events

font particular shape of letters used in printing

illustration picture that is drawn or painted

illustrator person who makes illustrations

imagination power of the mind to form pictures and ideas

nonfiction type of writing that describes real people and events

photographer person who takes photographs

picture researcher person who searches for pictures, especially photographs

printing company business (company) that prints the pages of books and magazines

publishing company business (company) that creates books and magazines

warehouse building where things are stored

Book Quiz

1. Is this book a fiction or a nonfiction book? (See page 4.)

2. Who usually has the idea for a nonfiction book? (See page 9.)

3. Who writes the outline? (See page 12.)

4. Who lays out the pages? (See page 18.)

5. What country was this book printed in? (See page 20.)

Find Out More

This cartoon guide shows how a children's fiction book is made:
www.penguin.co.uk/static/misc/uk/puffin/makebook3.swf

See a printing machine at work—it's noisy!
www.youtube.com/watch?v=MR-CbgKZwhE&feature=related

Answers

1. nonfiction, 2. the editor, 3. the author, 4. the designer, 5. China

Index